I Wanna Write
A Poem

by The Poor Man's Poet

1st run released November 2017 Hampton Roads, Virginia

copyright
1st edition Nov. 2017 ISBNs-13: 978-1978118973/-10: 197811897X
2nd edition 2020 **ISBN: 978-10952773-09-9**

contents

LIVING

Time	7
I Wanna Write a Poem	9
The Age of Indolence I	11
The Last Word (The Age of Indolence II)	15
Father's and Daughters	17
Mother Said	19
Bobby's Mom Don't Play	21
As A Poet	23
Before I Go On	25
Curves for Days!	27
The Visit	29
She Didn't Know	31
The Adventures of Captain Morgan	33
Nobody Cares	37
Homebody Cares	39
The Fashion Police	41
Lucky	43
Fortunately	45
Commonsense	47

It's Rough Being a Black Man   49

Today!   51

Tears   53

Color Lines   55

Gridlock   57

Just Not Your Year   59

Pressed Into Faith   61

Whoop Ass Delivery Service   63

My Brother   67

LOVING

All the Refreshment   71

Thirst   73

I Dreamed   75

I Dare to Dream   77

If Love Were a Fight   79

They Speak Of You   81

Five Feet of Paradise   83

Tabitha My Love   85

LIVING

Time

As Dawn begins to glow
every day performance,
every moment a show.
With a pen in my hand
the ink starts to flow.

Awakened by Epiphany
The daughter of Poetry.
Her whisper of inspiration
brings pen and pad to mind.
And I… Have time.

Early in the morning,
under the nighttime skies,
I'm there to see the sunrise.

There…
As morning glories creep.
I'm there…
As crickets go to sleep.
Before the darkness
says goodnight.
Before the first rays
of sunlight.
I… Have time…

I Wanna Write a Poem

I wanna write a poem about,
how in God we trust.
About getting our piece of the pie,
and eating the crust.
I wanna write a poem about,
Opportunity knocking on your door,
and learning to be careful
what you wish for.
I wanna write a poem about,
going to work and coming home alone,
and although you don't know anyone,
you hope there's messages on your phone.
About going out, meeting someone,
getting married having kids,
and wishing you were a lone poem.
I wanna write a poem about,
people with a kind heart,
how God put you in there way
and them doing their part.
I wanna write a poem about,
being in a room full of fine women.
Perfume in the air...
And the happy feeling I get,
because my wife isn't there...
I wanna write a poem about,
women who really understand,
that men are the weaker sex,
and will perform on demand.
I wanna write a poem about,
having no fear of the dark,
walking the streets alone
making it on our own.

And I wanna write a poem about
the homeless actually finding a home.
I wanna write a poem.
...
I wanna write a poem.

The Age of Indolence I

Being a household hero
and laying in my hammock,
is the only reason.
Summer in my backyard,
is my favorite season.
I love a soft warm southern breeze.
As I lay I the shade of red dogwood trees...
The only hurricane in the forecast,
is swirling with ice in my tall glass.
As I enjoy the lay of the land,
lounging here all day is only part of my plan.
Quietly protecting the peace,
my silent sentinel of serenity.
Man's best friend, a full grown
three-pound chocolate chi-hua-hua
asleep under my feet.
A beautiful woman enters my view,
and she has a list of chores for me to do.
Seeing the way, she's dressed and
headed in my direction I thought
maybe she'd like to help me
with my now rising (wish it was bigger).
She strolls toward me singing my name.
She sings a song of why I'm at the top of her list
for the lazy man's hall of fame.
Her velvety voice is music to my ears.
If you like the sound of a drill sergeant,
commanding troops for a number of years.

It is from my lovely wife
where I catch hell.
Because she knows her husband,
does nothing very well.

A wonderful woman, soft as silk,
but when she's in a mood her voice
has been known to curdle milk.
Lift that bail! tote that barge!
Trim those bushes! And wash the Car!
She says
Honey when are you going to cut the grass?
And I say
Right now, my riding mower seems to be out of gas.
She says
then you could put together the new barbecue grill.
I pictured the unopened box in my garage,
and say
Honey I checked the parts and its missing a wheel.
She says
OK! *When are you going to start building the back deck?*
And I said
Yesterday I talked to a contractor but he wouldn't take a check.
She says
The grand kids are looking forward
to playing on the new swings.
And I said
Well I think I'll have that together
by some time, next spring.
She says
Well *when are you going to walk this ole dog*
that pays me no mind?
And I said
If you look honey she's got four legs
and I think she walks just fine.
She says
you can at least wash the car and trim the bushes!

I take a sip from my drink,
and took a half minute to think...
I looked in her beautiful brown eyes.
Knowing this isn't what she wants to do.
She climbs into my arms, you see,
my hammock is very comfortable.
It was made for two.

The Last Word
(The Age of Indolence part II)

But I should have known she wasn't through.
She snuggled close to whisper in my ear,
and said I have a message for you.
She sounded sexy and sultry and licked my ear.
Cuddling with me,
I had both hands full of my favorite parts of her.
You're lucky I love you lazy old man. So listen here!
I'm not going to fool around with you
until your yard work is through.
I had a talk with the contractor about
the swing set and the back deck.
He said they can start next weekend
so I stroked the check.
I love my grandchildren and I love you,
don't ever make me choose between them or you.
If you don't start teaching this little dog to do what I say,
She's going to wake up in a shelter run by the S. P. C. A.
When I ask you to trim the bushes
and you smile like the dirty old man you are,
this time it won't get you very far.
Now as for helping you with your (wish it was bigger,)
I think we fit just right, and we're going to try
something new tonight.
Now get your hands off me
and go wash that filthy car.

Father's and Daughters

Daughters hold a special place
in our hearts.
As fathers we love playing our part.
Watching them grow and change
like the phases of he moon.
When they're upset with us
the tears fall like a Monsoon.
But we like to keep them happy
and I swear the sun shines when she smiles.
We look forward to giving a daughter
that push they need to move out on their own.
Then we both look forward to and dread
when they ring the phone.
As grown men we won't admit it,
Some times we need it,
to hear their voice
something inside us melts like ice cream
on a hot summer day.
The phone rings and she says
                     Hi Daddy! I'm Ok!

Mother Said

My Mother said you need to read
more than Comic books.
I know I'm not the only one.
Some of everything that I read
from my childhood to adult
has been made into movies.
Like Hollywood had nothing better to do
Than to follow me around,
every time I Pick up a book.
Someone picked up a phone.
What is he reading?
The Avengers, X-men and Dr. Strange
My Mother, who was an English Major,
said Bobby since you hate English in school,
you'll probably end up being a poet.
But you need to read more than Comic books.
I read and collected both DC and Marvel comic books.
In 1968 I was in the 5th grade
at public school No. 6
when my teacher Mr. Gamble read
the Lord of the Rings to the class.
I surprised my mother
When she caught me reading The Hobbit
Grow up and I joined the Army
Got sent overseas on hardship tour
Pulling guard duty I had a lot time on my hands.
So I read the books of Tom Clancy.
Hollywood found my reading list.
Hunt for the Red October, Patriot Game,
Clear and Present Danger.

Everything that I read from my childhood
To adult has been made into movies,
but I've also read books on massage
and you should know
those are x-rated movies.

Bobby's Mom Don't Play

You read that back in the day
studies have shown that you,
were one of the many.
But compared to today's kids
you, were one of the few.
You don't know how bad you were as kids
until you're grown.
And see how other kids behave out in public.
We got our asses toe up
on a regular basis.
I do mean almost every day.
I thank the Lord
my mother was the right
person for the job.
She was a disciplinarian.
You didn't get just three or four licks,
my mother made it worth her while
to whup your ass.
She whupped ass
like there was an award
for best ass whopping.
And there were punishments too.
Like you were grounded, no TV,
you had stay in your room
and read a book.
Or maybe you couldn't go outside for
a couple of weeks.
(There was no internet or cable.)
I turned out very well,
I am none the worse for wear.
And I do mean I wore
a lot of painful leather.

Or should I say my mother
wore out a lot leather on us.
As we were growing up
my mother went from using
belts to extension cords to
breaking brooms on us.
As a teenager, the best thing
she did was punch me in the mouth.
Right in front of my friends.
I had pick that moment
to talk back to her outside.
My friends talked about it for a year.
Your friends never let you forget,
they would say hey man,
was you there when Kinard's Mom
punched him in the mouth?
Man, Bobby's Mom don't play.

As A Poet

As a poet
You have the right
to remain silent.
If you give up that right.
Anything you say,
can and will be used
in the court
of public opinion.
You have the right
to use a computer keyboard.
If you cannot afford one,
a pen with a piece of paper
will be provided for you.
You have the right
to speak like an attorney,
to take your readers
on a trip or journey.
Giving them a feeling
of anticipation.
Using words out of
context or connotation,
or use long words
like conversation.
You have the right
to give your feelings a voice,
to express yourself in every
kind and category of poetry.
You can put together your own
musical group like the one called Floetry.
You have the right
to recite, day or night.
To speak out loud
in front of a crowd,

to make yourself heard!
With the freedom
of the spoken word!
To stand and proclaim,
to entertain,
Or choose the words
to describe your pain!
You, have the right to complain.
Know that for you,
No subject is taboo.
Only season your words with grace,
for you may have to eat them,
should someone throw them back in your face.

Before I Go On

Tonight's open Mic. at the coffee house.
I stand here waiting my turn.
Adrenaline has my heart is pounding,
and my stomach burns.
My nervous fear at showing fear.
Has me full of nervous fear.
From the middle of my gut
to the soles of my feet.
I wish I could leave fear at the door
when I walked in off the street.
The place is packed with a nice crowd,
my words are trying hard
to burst out loud.
A poet is speaking, one has already spoken,
I see a first timer who needs some air.
It's not his turn yet but he's already choking.

The mood in the room is like
a leaky dam that's about to give way.
The moderator says next on Mic.,
The Poor Man's Poet Bobby K.

From the back of the room
Like a wizard of spoken word,
speaking aloud so I can be heard.
Making my way to the microphone,
I mix motion with metaphor,
and like Merlin I make magic.

I walk like an Egyptian and speak like a king,
while I'm on the mic.
I feel like a boxing champ stepping into the ring,
With each word, I show no fear.

25

Roaring like a wild African lion
I am like a Zulu warrior hurling a spear.

Once again, I make my point
I drop a poem that cracks concrete,
my next piece is about women,
beautiful soft and sweet.
From the moment, I spoke up
until I sat down.
I am the mighty mouth,
one smooth human sound.
Everyone dealt with the fact
that the stage was mine,
until I gave it back.

Curves for days!

A sight for sore eyes
don't need no Visine.
Nothing you'd find in
thin, petite, skinny.
Not even small or lean,
we like'em thick
in them jeans.
Curves!
If ya know what I mean,
like a walking wet dream.
Curves for days!
Thick and sexy
thighs for my eyes.
Plus size, Voluptuous,
Big beautiful women.
Round in all the right places.
From there soft sumptuous lips
down to the soft sway of their hips.
Look at that
P-H-A-T FAT!
Beauty is in the eye
Men will stop traffic
at rush hour
just to watch
them walk by.
My My My!

The Visit

Hey!! wake up!! You don't wanna miss this!!
The soft voice that woke him, he didn't know.
Opening his eyes and seeing two grim faces.
Along with one that was angry and beautiful.
And the startling fact
the last thing he heard
was the Hammer being pulled back.
Click Click Click
None of them were family or kin,
never mind the question of how they got in.
Waking up to cold steel touching his skin.
But wait! This is not where the story begins.
A young no talent rapper, pimp wanna be,
just turning twenty three.
Running the streets trying to be somebody.
Not a member of a gang speaking nothing but slang.
using every four letter word except B-E-L-T.
That he needs to hold up the jeans hanging off his behind.
Thinking he's fine and in fashion
and always looking for some action.
Got the hook up and now carrying
a black 38 Smith & Wesson.
The young blood is in need of a good lesson.
Saw a beautiful young lady
and not wanting to miss a chance for a little romance.
He showed the lady the caliber of his conversation.
Of coarse she was not impressed.
But asked for his phone number.
Saying playfully you'll be hearing from me.
And well you know the rest.
Hey!! Wake up!! You don't wanna miss this!!
Click Click Click

She Didn't Know

I had my plan memorized, and I picked the right time.
I walked into the bank when there was no line.
I walked up to the teller and presented a note.
She hadn't lived my life, ya see I was going for broke.
With a white painter's cap,
matching sweat suit, and nice sneakers.

I thought I could have passed for a rapper,
but I was a thug wanna be.
This bank didn't have a guard
so, for me, the money was free.

The way she looked at the note
I could tell she wasn't impressed.
See I wrote it with an orange crayon
and well... I did my best.
That's when I unzipped my jacket,
to show her the sticks of dynamite
duck-taped to my chest.
I pulled out an old cell phone,
extended the small antenna just for effect.
I said lady, this is my first bank job,
I've never done this before.
I'll take all the money you have in the top drawer.
She saw my finger on the button,
I was in control,
and didn't wanna get caught by the local patrol.
Knowing I'm going to be on TV.
The lead on all the news channels.
She didn't know, with these road flares and old cell phone
I couldn't blow out a candle.

She gave me two bags of money, that felt good in my hands.
Then I made my get away, it was all part of the plan.
I didn't drive, and some will think on foot I won't get far.
But the cops are on their way,
so, I'll finish this poem on another day...

The Adventures of Captain Morgan

Well, it all started when
Jim Beam bet Jack Daniels
that Captain Morgan
couldn't go out
and get himself
some Wild Turkey.
Old Fashioned, like Old Granddad,
Captain Morgan like some of you,
really enjoys his Southern Comfort.
But mostly in the form of a woman named Wild Irish Rose.
It being near Thanksgiving and on most mornings,
you can hear the Wild Turkey's bird call.
For those of you who don't know,
the Wild Turkey's bird call
sounds just like a Screaming Orgasm.
Captain Morgan was out early
passing through the Angry Orchard
when he saw his friend Strongbow.
Strongbow, a native to these parts,
was already on the hunt for the Wild Turkey
and had one in his sights.
Just as he was drawing his bow
to take his shot,
there was a noise, a snort.
In a clearing right outside the Angry Orchard,
A Matador was mixing it up with a Red Bull.
And it was hard to tell who was winning.
When Captain Morgan and Strongbow looked again,
That Wild Turkey was gone...
Leaving tracks in two directions.
And a Screaming Orgasm could be heard in the distance.
Captain Morgan followed one set of tracks
and Strongbow the other.

Hot on the trail of that Wild Turkey
Captain Morgan ran into Smirnoff.
Smirnoff was headed over to Boone's Farm
to get himself some Grey Goose for breakfast.
Smirnoff said that Ron Bacardi
took Strawberry Daiquiri home
to meet his Bahama Mama.
Later he planned to show her his Mojito.
Jose Cuervo had taken Pena Colada
to Margarita Ville because he likes the way
she makes his Tequila Sunrise.
Now while all you alcoholics
are thinking about your favorite drink right now.
Captain Morgan met up with Johnny Walker
and his dog Whiskey crossing
Firewater Creek.
They stop to watch the Cognac Brothers
Courvoisier, Hennessy, & Remy Martin
work together to help Samuel Adams
Who was trapped on the Natural Ice.
Grateful for help, Samuel Adams thanked everybody.
And offered to buy a round of Pale Ale or some
Mike's hard Lemonade
He even told Captain Morgan that
he got stuck on the Natural Ice
when he stop to watch Elijah Craig
trying to help Brandy show off
her Fuzzy Naval.
Then tried to cover her Buttery Nipples
Using Pabst Blue Ribbon.
But Brandy was wearing Pabst Blue Ribbon
as part of her Bikini to cover her Heineken.
Brandy got her bikini caught on a Bud Light
when she jumped out the way
of a Rolling Rock when some

Rumrunners were hauling some Moonshine.
Now just when it started to look like
Jim Beam was going to collect
on that bet with Jack Daniels
Captain Morgan's cell rang.
It was Chardonnay.
Chardonnay rings his cell phone
every other day,
when she's ready to play!

Chardonnay said that
Cooking Sherry is barbecuing a wild turkey
she caught doing the funky chicken
in my backyard.
And that she's having a cookout
in her backyard.
With her girlfriends
Merlot, Reunite, Tequila Rose and Chianti.
And they all wanted to know
If he'd like to come get some?
Now!!... Will he get some Wild Turkey?
You better believe it.

Nobody Cares

Somewhere, Anywhere and Everywhere
Everybody's looking for somebody
and nobody cares.
Busybody told Everybody
that Somebody was trying
to get there freak on.
Nobody told Busybody
that Somebody likes to sleep till noon.
So, Busybody lied and told Everybody
that Somebody sleeps in the nude.
So, Everybody knocked on Anybody's door
looking for Somebody.
Anybody got mad
and told Everybody
where they can go,
Somebody knew that Busybody
was a gossip queen.
So, by the time
Everybody got there.
Somebody slapped Busybody
into next week...
Anybody could have stopped it
and told Nobody.
Nobody felt sorry for Busybody
because, Nobody cares...
Everybody reading this poem
knows Somebody like Busybody.
...
So, who cares?

Homebody Cares

Everybody knocked on Homebody's door,
Everybody said hi I'm looking for Somebody.
Homebody told Everybody that
Somebody went shopping with her cousins
Somewhere, Anywhere and Everywhere.
Everybody left looking for Somebody.

If Busybody was a gossip queen,
Then Homebody is a match maker,
Trying to fine a match for Anybody.
Anybody who's sexy and sassy
and a walking wet dream.
But Homebody was more than a pretty face
being thick and sexy.
Both of them were single and on the market,
Only Nobody was available.

Busybody told Nobody that he should
go out with Homebody,
But she can be a little bougie.
Nobody said that he's not picky,
that he'd even go out with Anybody.

Somebody knocked on Busybody's door
looking to have more than a few words.
Meanwhile Homebody was taking a shower
and then she put on some not-for-company clothes.
There was knock at the door,
Homebody yelled come in thinking it was Anybody.
And Nobody showed up with flowers and chocolate.
Nobody came looking for Anybody
He looked around and didn't see Anybody.

So Nobody asked Homebody
if she'd like dinner and a movie?
Homebody found a reason to get out the house.
And Everybody is still looking for Somebody.

The Fashion Police

You've always wanted
to call the fashion police.
Now you can!
When you're shocked
by what you see.
So many things come to mind,
people post them on Facebook
all the time.

People wearing things
that are supposed to be daring
but are just plain indecent.
To short, to tight
just don't look right.
Showing all of their ignorance.

Dial 1-800 take that off.
For those who don't know to dress
for the ladies wearing much too less.
Those who should be ashamed.
When poor choice and bad taste
are not to blame.

The Fashion Police
are there to enforce good taste.
Empowered by fashion experts
and your personal opinion.

Their motto is
Just because it comes in your size
don't mean you should wear it.
We've all seen it before,
things that should be left in the store.

Dial 1-800 take that off
The Fashion Police have the power to
capture, arrest and re-dress offenders on sight.
Any one, any time day or night.
The Fashion Police!
Will charge those who let them
come outside the house looking like that.
With conspiracy to commit embarrassment.

Call the fashion police
for cases of fashion disasters.
For old people who dare to go bare.
To help those with
wardrobe malfunctions.
For people who don't know
their wardrobe is
Out of style and tacky.

When needed the Fashion police
can call on their SWAT team.
To deal with bad hair cuts or hair do's
and ugly tattoo's.
For needed closet raids
confiscating retro and throw backs.
They will even take you in
for retail therapy.

Lucky

Lucky, I don't work for you,
for I would only kill you
with kindness.

But I would kill you
all the same.
I would kill you
on a daily basis.
And your children
will never know my name.

Lucky, I don't work for you,
I would never miss a day!
Fore killing you with kindness,
I would even go out of my way.

The other people
who work for you
and I hope this
never come to pass.
Because the other people
who work for you,
could be a lion
waiting in the tall grass.
Lucky.

Fortunately

Fortunately this family friendly function
finds me festive and not feisty in my fifties.
Forgive me if I am not the first
and you may have figured out
that the fact finding letter "F"
is my favorite letter
of the alphabet.
There are three thousand words
that start with the letter "F"
to which one hundred and ninety one
are four letter words.
And like most of us,
coming from a foul mouth family
I'm pretty sure we used
everyone of them.
This is not football,
you must be full of fiber and feces
if you think I'm going to fumble.
If you're looking for an F bomb
just look under your seats.
Now! When it comes to women.
My fanatic fantasies and fascination
of the fine figures of the female form.
My favorite fun loving fiancee
who I met at a Fountain
was the final finish of a fetish.
Where I use to
find'em fix'em and forget'em.

Commonsense

Lets be practical,
if commonsense
was as common
as its suppose to be.
Then it would make sense
For lots of people to use it.
We're all human and
Commonsense is something
to be used but never abused.
But some people
are deaf dumb and blind
when it comes to commonsense.
Like old people with selective hearing.
Ignoring good advice
Trying to share their native wit,
and you know they are
the definition of nit wit.
They like to think
that there are being shrewd
and you're trying hard not to be rude.
But they tend
to get on our last nerve
so we pull no punches.
We manage to call them
a whole mouth full of names.
Like stupid, ignorant, dents
and dimwitted.
Now they've brought you
down to their level,
you even lost a few
I.Q. Points,
commonsense says
you should walk away.

For them commonsense
is a woman screaming
in a sound proof room.
If commonsense had a voice
what would it say?
That I'm tired of being
ignored from day to day.

Commonsense
says a lot of things.
But no one has heard it speak.
I'm sure this makes sense to someone.

It's Rough Being a Black Man

It's rough being a black man
having no plan.
A victim of economic segregation
because you have no experience
or enough education.

It's tough being a black man
Your only claim to fame
is your God given ghetto name.
Rap star, no talent wanna be,
getting cut from the team,
killing any hope
of an N.B.A. Or N.F.L. dream.
So, you start hustling
selling drugs on the street.
You gotta compete
to stay on your feet.
But it's illegal how you
make ends meet.
You put in applications everywhere
few people are buying
and nobody's hire-ing.

It's rough being a black man
when your woman doesn't understand.
All of what it takes to be a man.
She tries to relieve her stress and strife
telling you how rough it is being
a black woman, let alone your wife.
But your patience is barely contained
tired of hearing her complain.

You know she's not alone,
she's caring for your child,
you gotta bring more money home.

It's rough being a black man
when you fail to plan, you plan to fail.
Everyday opportunities passing you by.
Taking you further from your dream
of living large, never mind just getting by.
You take a second look up into the sky,
you wanna ask God please tell me why?
It's rough being a black man.
The two of you manage
to get a half way decent job,
putting your pennies together,
and damned if you don't get robbed.
When Uncle Sam takes his cut
of what you call a pay check.

You wanted to get away from it all,
the hustle and street crime of the city.
Making a poor decision
Moving to a suburb or subdivision.
Trying to get ahead before
and you end up in jail
or maybe even dead.
Because you were followed
by the police who
don't understand.
The trouble starts with
let me see your hands.
It's rough being a black man

Today!

It's the new kid at work,
a fresh hire right from the street.
And for about a week I heard the brother speak.
I was offended, especially since he was long winded.
I didn't want to take him to church,
Because I didn't want to preach.
But I felt there was a lesson that I needed to teach.
I wanted to give him a goal,
something he could reach.
I wanted to give him a better command
of his freedom of speech.
I said hey man, for about a week
I couldn't help but hear you speak.
You with your colorful vocabulary
the way you talk about friends and family.
So, let me ask you.
Can we not be Niggas today?
Would you stop using that term
that makes my ears burn.
Can we not be Niggas today?
Everything and everybody
that was moving stopped...
You could have heard a pin drop.
He looked at me like I had attacked him,
it was just a simple request.
But he stood back like I smacked him.
He said, Man! Don't nobody talk like you!
I said, Now that's not true,
and I don't remember asking for your point of view.
I may speak out turn which makes me rude,
but you've been speaking out ignorance,
And that my brother makes you kind of crude.
So, can we not be Niggas today?

You're suppose to a role model for your kids
a beacon of intelligence,
but you sound like the victim
of an educational system's negligence.
Can we not be Niggas today?
Why do we have to be Niggas anyway?
We are a people of Trailblazers,
Innovators and Entertainers.
We are creative and lite on our feet,
we hustle and handle are business,
making money on the street.
We are some of highest paid professional athletes.
We are Runner's Rapper's and Readers,
We are Poets, Preachers and Teachers,
We are Layers, Lovers and Leaders.
We are Presidents and Vise-Presidents of corporations.
We as a people, our generation,
made history when we voted
the first black man to run this nation.
I hope you can understand my indignation.
and feel my frustration
I know there are so many better
things you can say!
Just so long as We...!
Are Not Niggas Today!

Tears

Here in America, African Americans,
well I should say on unarmed black people.
It's always been open season.
They don't need a hunting licensee
all they need is a police uniform.
They have been killing us for years
only to be matched
by a Mothers pain and tears.
What needs to go out of style,
is the policeman's use of a racial profile
If all the police carried Nothing but nonlethal weapons.
Nationwide there would be more days where nobody died.
The media would have to find something else to sensationalize.
In time, we can forgive but never forget,
put the past behind us and pray
they don't make us regret.
It might be possible to for both sides
to have mutual respect.
But for now, I won't take that bet,
Because some white people won't let it go.
Those with little or no economic advantage
who can't afford to move.
Feel that they are stuck living with us
and there goes the neighborhood.
Not all of our young men are living the street life.
A number of us get good jobs and a wife.
No! we are not the Huxtables, we are income adjustable.
Some of us are the epitome of cool
doing our thing and going to school.
Promising Olympic athletes,
future Pro-Baseball, Basketball or Football stars.
Living the life only to fall victim
to a drive by shooting or a mugger with a knife.

Black on black crime is still in fashion,
some of us are tired of getting their daily ration,
we need to stop the violence, stop all that action.
The Justice system and jail
have a revolving door. Need I say more.

Color Lines

Thanks to all those brave souls,
the trail blazers
that have gone before us.
They, who fell in love,
back when white society
wasn't so accepting or
was intolerant of mixed marriage.
Love is made of tough stuff,
couples had it ruff.
So, for a while, some lovers even
kept a low profile.
This has been going on for a long while.
But they took a leap of faith anyway,
staying to themselves.
Love will not be denied.
They don't need to hide.
Now days you see mixed couples everywhere...
Not just in and around military bases.
Today it's not a shock,
but a pleasant surprise.
Seeing couples from two different cultures,
people from around the world
and even different size.
Both straight and gay,
more than just black and white.
As day follows night,
all kinds of races mixing it up.
My coworker married a Mexican
she is Cambodian and they have
three of the most beautiful daughters.
One has only to open your eyes to see,
the mixing of the of the melting pot,
which is hot.

Love truly conquers all.
God is in control,
He has taken the spoon
and stirred the melting pot,
from the top of the rim
to the bottom of the bowl.

Gridlock

Rolling down the highway,
We all feel the urgency
of morning rush-hour.
everybody in flight.
Vehicle lights,
a flowing river
of red and white.

New vehicles are
ergonomic and aerodynamic.
Rush-hour feels like
a controlled panic.
Impatient people
with a gas pedal,
sets the stage for road rage.
They cut it close
when they cut you off,

You lay on the horn
because they must be insane.
You call them a whole
mouthful of names.
Your wish is granted
as they breakdown in
the passing lane.
Smiling as you look up
in your rear-view mirror.
To your hearts desire
their engine is a blaze,
damn thing caught on fire.

People not paying attention
almost causing a wreck.
As traffic begins to bottleneck.
It takes time to slow down
and go around.
Like it or not
they're caught in the gridlock.
Their fastest route to work or home
just became a parking lot.

Just Not Your Year

Life is full of surprises,
as you recognize your fear.
An adrenaline fueled
fight or flight puts your ass in gear.

You'd like to think
That you are brave.
You have no problem
Facing fear.
But you have a funny feeling
That 2017
Is just not your year.

Cleaning up the back yard
In the springtime
Trying not to get stung by a wasp.
A snake comes out of nowhere
And you break camp like a boss.

Shouting oh Lord!
As your skin starts to crawl.
Luck for you it's a baby
But to you it doesn't look that small.
You step back for a moment.
When you step forward again
It's the middle of fall.

Raking leaves
In the front yard
Waving hello to your
Lovely neighbor.
And she really looks fine,

Breaking his chain, her
Vicious Rottweiler has
Something else in mind.
Your feet start moving
Before your brain knows what to do.
If you get bit
By her vicious Rottweiler
You and your good intentions are through…
Moving with a practiced ease.
You're faster than a cool breeze.
You thank the Lord for the little things
Like how vicious Rottweilers
Can't climb trees.

You like to think that you are brave.
You have no problem facing fear.
But you have a funny feeling
That 2017 is just not your year.

Pressed Into Faith

I guess she wasn't good enough
for that little man.
when my parents were having words,
My Father would give my Mother the back of his hand.
It's not with her husband my mother wanted to fight.
Because she knew, he was listening to his mother
who always thought she was right.
I guess she wasn't good enough for that little man.
I don't know, backhanding my mother
may not have been part of grandmother's plan.
But what happened the next time
made me my mother's number one fan.
Now I was too young to witness this.
My mother told me about it years later.
She even showed me the clipping from the newspaper.
She was ironing his shirts for work one day
and they were having words their same old way.
He turned to backhand her like he would usually do.
But she grabbed his hand before he could follow through.
She... ironed a wrinkle on his shoulder
and another one on his chest,
manage to get his midsection as he hollered and professed.
He tried to get away, but stumbled and fell.
It's a good thing he found religion,
because he sure caught hell.

The article in the paper read "Black man pressed into faith"
after receiving second and third degree burns
from his irate wife with an iron.
It was reported the husband heard the calling of the Lord.
The police were called, and a local news reporter
had made it there too.

She explained to them both, in defending herself.
"I had reached my limit, I did what I had to do.
I changed my husband's attitude with an iron,
and he's going to need some help removing my shoe.
I mean I couldn't take any more.
So, I whupped him and kicked his sorry ass out the door."
Being an abused woman, my mother hadn't quite recovered.
if one ever does.
When I read the newspaper clipping
it gave me an ah-ha moment.
When I was a lot younger
I made the mistake of slapping my sister
right in front of my mother, and my mother lost it.
As far as she was concerned, I must be ready to die.
She did in this order, tried to kill me, skin me alive,
and hang me out to dry.
While she was ringing my neck,
she said what mothers said back then.
(Boy I brought you into this world, and I'll take you out!)

Whoop Ass Delivery Service

It's when you don't have
the money for a hit man.
And you know something
needs to be done.
If you have a hot date
and your boss asked you
to work late.
Dial 1-800 Whoop that ass
if a loved one
doesn't know how to come home,
or people who get smart
with you on the phone.
Hang up and dial
Dial 1-800 Whoop that ass.

For someone who needs
their ass handed to them.
The old fashion way.
Let us do that for you.
Dial 1-800 Whoop that ass.

The Whoop Ass Delivery Service
We will deliver a can of whup ass
anywhere to anyone at any time
day or night, if they're wrong or right,
in any kind of weather.
Call and ask about
the wet ass whupping
for no extra charge.

On your request, we can leave them
on their feet or
laying on the ground.
We can deliver a can of whup ass
in public or when no one's around.

Satisfaction Guaranteed
or we will tear dat ass up.

Dial 1-800 Whoop that ass.
The Whoop Ass Delivery Service
let's you choose one of three sizes
The Small, (This is gonna hurt)
The Medium, (We're gonna break something)
and The Large. (Put them in the hospital)

Each package comes with fightback insurance.
Just in case the subject tries to fight back
In which case
we will beat the snot out them.
Ladies if you wanna
keep your abusive husband in line,
then keep us in mind.
Dial 1-800 Whoop that ass.

Ladies our slap happy option
comes as a back-hand service.
Where at you request.
we can just slap the piss
out of them.
Slap the taste out they mouth.
Slap the shit out of them.
Or even slap them into next week.
Dial 1-800 Whoop that ass.

And men we don't discriminate,
We can return the favor for a nominal fee.
We will slap people on both sides
of the family tree.
Dial 1-800 Whoop that ass.

We take Visa, Master card, American Express
Don't let credit problems get in the way!
You can even put an Ass Whooping on Lay-away.
Find us online at any time. @WhoopthatAss.com

My Brother

My brother had his friends
and I had mine.
We were playing
in a tree that was
easy to climb.
He was showing off
jumping from limb to limb
only this time he missed
and I watched him fall.
One bone is broken
his pride was a little hurt.
Bad news for my mother
who just got off from work.

Like a hero
our friends carried him to my mother.
Who showed more anger than alarm?
Her ten-year-old showoff
had just broken his arm.
Didn't come to any real harm.
At least he wasn't bleeding
and hadn't broken his neck.
Sad now the Hospital
will be getting most
of my mother's small check.

LOVING

... Dedicated to Tabitha Ann Brown

All the Refreshment

If a man could drink
with his eyes,
then you are all
the refreshment
I could ever want or need.
Your skin is the color
of my coffee in the morning.
And as I kiss you with each sip.
It goes without saying...
I take my coffee black.
Savoring my second sip,
Caressing the surface
of your softness.
You're a one of a kind sensation
a refreshing rejuvenation.
For a lunch time lover
you give new meaning
to a midday martini.
I go through my day
wondering,
how can I be so lucky?
to fall in love with
a walking work of art.
It must be my calling
because I'm still falling.
You stay on my mind
you stay on my lips.
You stole my heart
long before this morning's first kiss.
You are my sweet chocolate escape.

As I come home
To the paradise of your warm embrace.
You're the love of my life.
And all the happiness I could ever want or need.

Thirst

I look for you
to quench my thirst.
You are like the finest wine
I most certainly deserve.
Your fragrance and soft serenity
surrounds you like a warm glow,
and like a moth to a flame.
I am drawn to you
like a husband coming home.
Falling into your arms,
I know I have found
my personal paradise.
I love the tenderness
of your embrace.

You are the sister of angels,
and I can see it in your face.
Your very beautiful eyes,
and those soft warm sweet lips,
and all the rest of you
that I have missed.
I have been waiting
my whole life,
for just your kiss.
And as we kiss
I'll take a sip
to sample your essence...
Savoring the flavor
of pleasure and bliss
that drips from our lips
like falling dreams...

Satisfying my soul
you're always first,
quenching more than my thirst
like a warm cloud burst
in the middle of a quiet storm.

I am lost in the moment
Caught by your caress.
Celebrating the taste
of ecstasies success...
I love this woman!
Giving me a refreshing squeeze
you mean more to me
than the air I breathe.
Holding you in my arms
I inhale your scent.
Closing my eyes in this moment...
I am content...
I Love this woman!

I Dreamed

I dreamed you were a poem
that has not been written.
A poem about you as an ocean.
No one has ever seen you so blue,
or measured the depths
of the beauty within you.
The way you enjoy
a pleasant unexpected surprise.
Or the feel of the morning sunrise.
Of spring time coming too soon.
Or the smell of all the flowers in bloom.
A moth freeing itself from winter's cocoon.
Takes flight by the light of a full moon.
A poem about you as a kiss
that caresses the soul.
An emotional poem where lover's lose control.
Like majestic mountain snow covered peaks!
A love exploring the heights of ecstasy's reach.
A provocative poem of wild parties
and never ending nights.
A passionate poem wondering
what if love were a fight?
A delicious poem of discovery and delight,
of lovers wishing for just one more night!
A poem that poets,
are still waiting to write...
I dreamed you were a poem
that has not been written.

I Dare to Dream

As I dare to dream,
a full-time fantasy,
a wonderful wet dream.
Perfect aspirations
of a single wish,
to start each day
with but a taste
of your lips.
I dare not go further
beyond perfect bliss.
For my desire demand, more
of what I wish.
If I could wrap myself
around you,
I would be content
as your skin.
Caressing the surface
of your softness.
Falling into your warm embrace.
I am lost in love...
Taken to another place.
Paradise is you and I
Where ever we are
there's no one
in the whole world
but us...
As I dare to dream,
I've never been to heaven...
Instead, I spent the night
with you.

If Love Were a Fight

I am not a violent person
in any physical way
but if love were a fight
I'd fight you this day.
If love were a fight,
I would fight you all night
under twinkling stars
by the full moon light.
If love were a fight
I'd fight you near the ocean
where the rolling weaves
are poetry in motion.
I'd fight you in the depths
of the deep blue sea.
As your lover, I'd fight you
for every moment
you spend with me.
If love were a fight
I'd fight you in the desert
as twilight sets fire
to the sun baked sands,
I'd fight you
across the mountain tops,
I hope you understand.
That I will never tire in my desire
or seek any rest.
For I will give it my all,
and fight you
with my last breath.
If love were a fight
I would show no mercy,
give no quarter,
respect no time line

demarcation or border.
I would kick Godzilla in the knees.
Call Goliath a punk.
Resurrect Houdini and leave
him trapped in a trunk.
If love were a fight
there is no limit to
what I would do.
But I would thank God,
I'm fighting with you...

They Speak Of You

Hey beautiful,
How often have I called you
softly by that name?
Your voice is a warm whisper
more soothing than a gentle rain.
You are lovely in so many ways,
I could spend eighty-eight days times eighty-eight ways,
just writing poems and plays.
Dedicated to just how beautiful you are.
From your head to your toes to your near perfect nose
and all your girly parts in between.
You have only to look in the mirror to see what I mean.
You are the beauty of a single sunflower
in the middle of a desert oasis,
as twilight sets fire to the sun baked sands.
You were made by the hand of God
and wanted by every man.
You are the beauty of a cool glass of water
on a world where summer is eternal,
and no one has had a drink in a thousand years.
What I believe to be true,
the word beautiful was invented for you.
So, when anyone, anywhere, at any time
utters the word beautiful, they speak of you.
Perfect in all your imperfections
you've been beautiful all your life.
And if it hasn't happened already,
one day some lucky young man,
is gonna beg you to be his wife.

For you're a natural beauty,
that kind of beauty
where make up makes no sense.
You're the answer to the question...
Why mess with perfection?

Five Feet of Paradise

One day when it feels right,
Tabitha's going to be my wife.
I don't have to think twice,
we love each other and
she's just that damn nice,
my Five Feet of Paradise.

She is my one and only vice.
The kids think we're putting on a show
because we kiss and hold hands everywhere we go.
Tabitha is my life's connection,
a walking public display of affection.
She is my affliction, my adopted addiction.
I am not looking for nor do I want a cure.
She's a healthy habit I don't want to break.
I love that woman more
than a fat kid loves cake.

Make no mistake!
Our love runs deeper
than the water in all five
of the great lakes.
I love her like a King should love a Queen.
I kiss her good night
only to see her in my dreams.
Our romance is like a never-ending love poem,
we're trying to find a house,
but Tabitha is my home.
And one day when it feels right,
Tabitha's going to be my wife.
We don't argue fuss or fight,
because with Tabitha
every night, is a good night.

We do what grown folks do
in the wee hours of the morning.
So, every morning, is a good morning.
My queen wears her dignity and confidence
like a crown, she just happens to be
the loveliest shade of brown.
Her beauty and good nature go hand in hand.
And I, am very happy to be her man.
Wherever she goes is where I want to be.
Five feet of paradise,
Tabitha Brown, and me.

Tabitha My Love

Tonight, our bedroom window
holds a view of a full moon.
I lay here happy, enjoying
the first night of our honeymoon.
watching the woman I love,
my sleeping beauty.
As moonlight plays on her soft silhouette.
Dirty brown hair, face half buried in a pillow.
She smiles elated in her desires,
after satisfying her lover and her ego.
Tabitha dreams in deep peaceful slumber.
Slowly, I peel away satin covers,
undressing her for the second time.
Caressing her shoulder with a tender touch,
I hear music in her laughter as she wakes.
Its amazing someone so lovely would have me.
She's lovelier than all the flowers of spring,
she's my darling diva.
Tabitha makes me feel like a king.
She is a star and I am her fan,
I am more than happy to be her man.
She truly has my heart.
A portrait of brown sugar,
Tabitha's a living work of art
painted...
By the hand of God.

colophone

Brought to you by Wider Perspectives Publishing, care of Tanya Cunningham and James Wilson with the mission of advancing the poetry and creative community of Hampton Roads, Virginia.

See our production of the works of
    Tanya Cunningham (Scientific Eve)
    Raymond M. Simmons
    Taz Waysweete'
    Bobby K. (The Poor Man's Poet)
    J. Scott Wilson (TEECH!)
    Sarah Eileen Williams
and others to come soon.

We promote and support the artists of the 757
from the seats, from the stands,
from the snapping fingers and clapping hands
from the pages, and the stages
and now we pass them forth to the ages

Stop it James, just stop it!

Check for the above artists on FaceBook, the Virginia Poetry Online channel on YouTube, and the Hampton Roads Artistic Collective webpage.
Hampton Roads Artistic Collective is the non-profit extension of WPP and strives to simultaneously support worthy causes in Hampton Roads and the creative artists.

This first collection by Bobby K., affectionately known as "The Poor Man's Poet," is divided seamlessly into two sections.

Bobby shares the workings of his heart with the skill of a storyteller and the excitement of a smitten suitor. He embraces faith and family with great care and a deft touch of humor.

We accompany Bobby K. on a journey that demonstrates the fragility of life and the joys that are gold nuggets worth recalling again and again.

– Ann Falcone Shalaski author of World Made of Glass & Without Pretense

The self-proclaimed, "Po' Man's Poet" is rich in lyrical presence. Bobby K is the poet that always has a great story to tell. His down to earth observations on love and everyday life combined with comic relief makes him, "Every Man's Poet" because he leaves the reader with a comfortable sense of being understood.

– Talya Chatman

.

www.ingramcontent.com/pod-product-compliance
Lightning Source LLC
Chambersburg PA
CBHW021625270326
41931CB00008B/879